Nelson
Spelling ②

Danila De Sousa

Series Authors

Danila De Sousa
Donna Duplak
Deb Kekewich
Jim Kekewich
Clare Kosnik
Louis Quildon
Edgar Schmidt
Catherine Walker

Clare Kosnik, Senior Author

I(T)P® Nelson

an International Thomson Publishing company

Toronto • Albany • Bonn • Boston • Cincinnati • Detroit • London • Madrid • Melbourne
Mexico City • New York • Pacific Grove • Paris • San Francisco • Singapore • Tokyo • Washington

I(T)P® **International Thomson Publishing**
    The ITP logo is a trademark under licence

Published in 1998 by
I(T)P® **Nelson**
A division of Thomson Canada Limited
1120 Birchmount Road
Scarborough, Ontario M1K 5G4
Visit our Web site at **http://www.nelson.com/nelson.html**

All rights in this book are reserved.

ISBN 0-17-606556-3

Canadian Cataloguing in Publication Data

De Sousa, Danila, 1972–
    Nelson spelling 2

ISBN 0-17-606556-3

1. Spellers.   2. English language – Orthography
and spelling – Problems, exercises, etc.   I. Title

PE1145.2.D47 1997   428.1   C97-93914-5

Team Leader/Publisher: Mark Cobham
Executive Editor: Susan Green
Project Editor: Jennifer Rowsell
Series Editor: Joanne Close
Series Designer: Peggy Rhodes
Cover Illustrator: Per-Henrik Gurth
Senior Composition Analyst: Marnie Benedict
Production Coordinator: Theresa Thomas
Permissions: Vicki Gould
Film: Imaging Excellence
Photography: Ray Boudreau

Printed and bound in Canada

Acknowledgements
Permission to reprint copyright material is
gratefully acknowledged. Every reasonable effort
to trace the copyright holders of materials
appearing in this book has been made.
Information that will enable the publisher to
rectify any error or omission will be welcomed.

"Homemade Boat" by Shel Silverstein from
WHERE THE SIDEWALK ENDS. Copyright ©
1974 by Evil Eye Music, Inc. Reprinted with
permission of HarperCollins Publishers; "What a
Day" by Shel Silverstein from WHERE THE
SIDEWALK ENDS. Copyright © 1974 by Evil
Eye Music, Inc. Reprinted with permission of
HarperCollins Publishers; Cover illustration by
Eric Carle reprinted by permission of Philomel
Books from THE VERY HUNGRY
CATERPILLAR, © 1969 by Eric Carle; "Be
Prepared" © 1990 Sonja Dunn from CRACKERS
AND CRUMBS. Reprinted with permission.
Pembroke Publishers, 538 Hood Road, Markham,
Ontario L3R 3K9 Canada; "Secrets" from *If You
Could Wear My Sneakers!* copyright © 1997 text
by Sheree Fitch, illustrations by Darcia Labrosse.
Reprinted with permission of Doubleday Canada
Limited; "As Far" by George Swede from
THERE WILL ALWAYS BE A SKY, Nelson
© 1993; "The Sun's Behind the Houses" by Loris
Lesynski, author/illustrator of BOY SOUP and
OGRE FARM.

Illustrators
The author and publisher gratefully acknowledge
the contributions of the following illustrators:
Sean Dawdy, Norman Eyolfson, Dusan Petricic,
and Sue Truman.

Reviewers
The author and publisher gratefully acknowledge the contributions of the following educators:

Diane Assinger   Lynne Healy   Josephine Scott
Red Deer, AB   Lower Sackville, NS   Guelph, ON

Deborah Braithwaite   Caroline Lutyk   Mary Tarasoff
Toronto, ON   Grimsby, ON   Victoria, BC

4 5 ITIB 02 01

Table of Contents

Lesson		Page

Lesson		Page

Extra-Challenge Lessons

About Your Nelson Spelling Book

Here are some notes about your book. It includes many parts that help you learn about words and become a better speller.

Lessons

Each lesson looks at 1 spelling pattern. It opens with a poem, a story part, or a picture. The opener has the lesson's spelling pattern.

2   br, fr, gr

Creating Your Word List

Each lesson has a Word Box that contains 8 words. Use these words, the opener, and other words that share the same pattern to make your Lesson Word list. These are the words you will learn to spell.

Word Box

bring
brother
brown
frog
from
green
grow
grass

Spelling Strategy

Strategy Spot

Say It Right

Saying a word correctly helps you spell it correctly. Say 1 Lesson Word correctly. Listen to the letter sounds in the word.

Zoom in on Your Words

Activities, puzzles, and games help you learn the meaning and spelling of your Lesson Words. In Zoom In On Your Words, you will practise your Lesson Words and learn new words.

Try This! is an extra challenge you may want to do.

Did You Know?

Some lessons include Did You Know? spots. These spots contain interesting information about words and their origins.

 At Home activities and games can be done on your own or with a family member.

 FLASHBACK

 A flashback question is included at the end of each lesson. It asks you to think about what you have learned.

FOCUS ON LANGUAGE ▷ Compound Words

These pages give information and activities on many topics. You can learn when to capitalize letters, what nouns and verbs are, and how to make your writing more exciting.

Connecting with...

Spelling is a part of all subjects. These pages include spelling information and activities in subjects such as math, art, science, and media.

Connecting with
SOCIAL STUDIES

Spell Check

After every 5 lessons, you will do a Spell Check lesson. These lessons review patterns and strategies you have been learning. You will use the Lesson Words you still need to practise in games, puzzles, and other activities.

Read this rhyme with a partner.

The Cat and the Fiddle

Hey, diddle, diddle!
The cat and the fiddle,
The cow jumped over the moon;
The little dog laughed
To see such a sport,
And the dish ran away with the spoon.

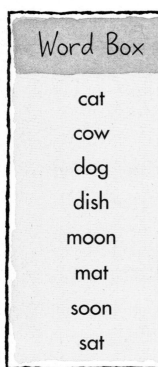

Word Box

cat

cow

dog

dish

moon

mat

soon

sat

Creating Your Word List

Say these words:

cat

dog

moon

sat

Which letters begin the words? Say the sound each letter makes.

1. List words that start with **c**, **d**, **m**, or **s**. Print your words in a chart like this one.

c	d	m	s

2. Use Word Box words, the rhyme, and the chart to make your list of Lesson Words.

3. **In your notebook**
   - Print your Lesson Words.
   - Circle the first letter in each word.

Strategy Spot

Learn About Spelling Strategies

A spelling strategy is a way to help you spell words. In each lesson, you will learn a new strategy.

Zoom in on Your Words

1. **Your Strategies** What do you do when you don't know how to spell a word? Tell a partner.

2. **Be an Artist** Choose 3 words from the rhyme. Draw a picture of each word. Label your pictures.

moon   cow   dog

3. Scrambled Words Unscramble these letters to spell Word Box words.

tas = sat

a) gdo   **b)** noos   **c)** dhsi

d) atm   **e)** woc   **f)** omon

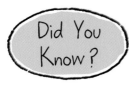

Did You Know? There are 26 letters in the alphabet. Most letters, like **c**, **d**, **m**, and **s**, are **consonants**. The other letters are **vowels** (a, e, i, o, u).

4. C, D, M, and S in the Classroom

Work with a partner. Write names of things in the class that begin with **c**, **d**, **m**, or **s**. Circle the first letter in each word and sound it out.

ⓓesk
ⓢeat
ⓒlock
ⓜat

5. At Home Write a list of things at home that begin with the letters **c**, **d**, or **s**.

FLASHBACK

What was your favourite activity in this lesson?

Connecting with

ART

Collages

A collage is made up of small pictures. Make a collage for 1 letter of the alphabet. Here are the steps:

1. Pick a letter.
2. Look through newspapers and magazines. Find pictures of words that start with this letter.
3. Cut out the pictures.
4. Draw your letter on a sheet of paper.
5. Put your pictures around the letter.
6. Glue the pictures. Wait for your collage to dry.

Try This! Make a book of collages with your classmates. Each page should have a different letter of the alphabet. Make sure they are in alphabetical order!

Would you like to be Ned?

A Bee

A B C D E F G
Do you see the darting bee?
H I J K L M N
See it hide inside the den
O P Q R S T U
Then under the kitchen table – it's brand new!
V W X Y and Z
Duck! Dodge! Now it's chasing Ned!

Creating Your Word List

Say these words:

day   under   bed

Look at the consonant **d**. See how it can be at the beginning, middle, or end of a word.

1. List words that have the consonant **d**. Print your words in a chart like the one on the next page.

Word Box

did

day

doll

under

hide

bed

Dad

said

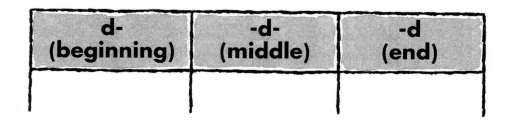

d- (beginning)	-d- (middle)	-d (end)

2. Use Word Box words, the rhyme, and the chart to make your list of Lesson Words.

3. In your notebook
- Print your Lesson Words.
- Circle the consonant **d** in each word.

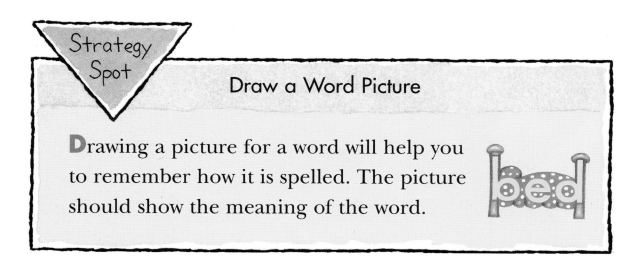

Strategy Spot

Draw a Word Picture

Drawing a picture for a word will help you to remember how it is spelled. The picture should show the meaning of the word.

Zoom in on Your Words

1. Word Pictures Choose 3 Lesson Words. Make a word picture for each word. Share your pictures with a partner.

2. Sound Clap Ask a partner to read your Lesson Words.

   a) Clap when you hear **d** at the **beginning** of a word.

   b) Snap your fingers when you hear **d** in the **middle** of a word.

   c) Stamp your feet when you hear **d** at the **end** of a word.

3. Find the Words Find Word Box words that complete these sentences.

It was a hot _ _ _. Toni and her _ _ _ sat _ _ _ _ _ the tree. "I know," _ _ _ _ her father. "Let's go for ice cream. It is the best thing we can do on a _ _ _ like this!"

4. At Home Read a favourite poem. Print words that have the letter **d**. Make a chart like the one on page 13.

FLASHBACK

Which activity helped you the most with your spelling?

FOCUS ON LANGUAGE
Alphabetical Order

A, B, C, D, E, F, G... all the way up to **Z**!
When words are in order from A to Z,
we say they are in alphabetical order.

Alphabetical order is used in

- dictionaries,
- some word lists (see page 126),
- telephone books.

Tamika put these words in alphabetical
order. Excellent, Tamika!

Make an alphabet strip.

1. Cut a strip of paper. It should be about 5 cm wide and 15 cm long.

2. Print the alphabet in order from A to Z.

3. Decorate your alphabet strip.

4. Place it where you can see it.

Judy must pick up words with the **short a** sound. Which words would you take?

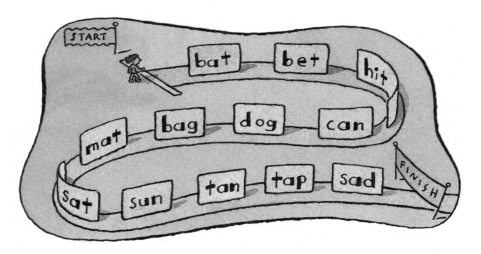

Word Box

at

hat

plan

sad

and

fast

man

add

Creating Your Word List

Say these words:

Listen to the sound of **short a**.

1. As a class, make a list of words that contain the **short a** sound.

2. Use the Word Box, picture, and class list to make your list of Lesson Words.

3. **In your notebook**
   - Print your Lesson Words.
   - Circle the letter that makes the **short a** sound in each word.

Use a Dictionary

A dictionary can help you spell words. It lists words in alphabetical order (**A** to **Z**). Here is how it works.

1. Jason wants to spell the word **plan**.

2. He finds the page with **p** words.

3. The next letter is **l** so he looks for words that begin with **pl**.

4. He finds his word. The dictionary also tells him the meaning of the word **plan**.

Zoom in on Your Words

1. Find Words in a Dictionary Look up 3 words you want to spell. Copy them in your notebook.

2. What's the Word? Use Word Box words to complete these groups.

      a) happy and _ _ _
      b) coat, boots, and _ _ _
      c) _ _ _ and subtract
      d) woman, child, and _ _ _

3. Fishing Trip! Work with a partner. Match each hook to the fish. Say each word you make. What is the same about the words?

4. At Home Look through old magazines and newspapers. Cut out words that have the **short a** sound. Use the words to make a collage.

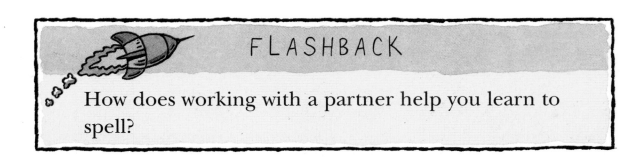

FLASHBACK

How does working with a partner help you learn to spell?

FOCUS ON LANGUAGE
Personal Dictionaries

A Personal Dictionary is your own dictionary. You decide which words to include.

1. You will need 27 pages in your dictionary.

2. Label the first page **A**. Label the second page **B**. Continue until you have labelled the last page **Z**.

3. Write a word on the left side of the page. You can draw a picture of your word on the right side of the page.

Rex needs a home. Would you like him as a pet?

Wanted – The Best Home
Rex is a lonely dog who needs a friend. He is ten months old. He enjoys pulling a sled and running. Rex needs to be fed two times a day. He would make a great pet!

Word Box

fed

peg

yes

pet

wet

get

ten

when

Creating Your Word List

Say these words:

fed   pet   when

Listen to the **short e** sound in each word.

1. As a class, make a list of words that contain the **short e** sound.

2. Use the Word Box, advertisement, and class list to make your list of Lesson Words.

3. In your notebook

- Print your Lesson Words.
- Circle the letter that makes the **short e** sound in each word.

Strategy Spot

Look, Cover, and Write!

Here is 1 way to study your Lesson Words.

1. Look at the word. Say it slowly.

2. Cover the word. Picture it in your mind.

3. Print the word.

4. Uncover the word. Check your spelling.

5. Print it again if you had trouble spelling the word.

Zoom in on Your Words

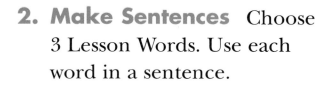

1. Look, Cover, and Write Use the strategy to practise 5 Lesson Words.

2. Make Sentences Choose 3 Lesson Words. Use each word in a sentence.

3. What's My Word? Trade Lesson Word lists with a partner. Choose 1 word. Give clues about the word. Your partner guesses the word. Take turns.

Try This! Your partner spells the word.

4. Word Wheel Imagine you can spin this wheel to make new words. Print each word you can make.

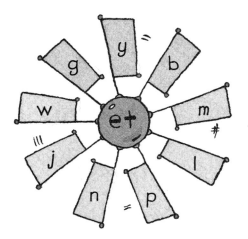

5. At Home Make a list of objects whose names have the **short e** sound. Bring the list to class.

FLASHBACK

Where do you keep your Personal Dictionary?

SOCIAL STUDIES

Your Classroom

Your classroom is a special place. Draw a poster to show interesting things in it. Jennifer's classroom looks like this:

1. Draw your classroom. Decide what you will include in your picture.
2. Colour it.
3. Label objects in your classroom. Make sure you spell them correctly. If you need help, look in the dictionary, ask a partner, or check with your teacher.

Have you been in a boat like this one?

Homemade Boat

This boat that we built is just fine –
And don't try to tell us it's not.
The sides and the back are divine –
It's the bottom I guess we forgot...

Shel Silverstein

Word Box
this
is
it
sit
pig
big
him
hit

Creating Your Word List

Say these words:

is   big   him

Listen to the **short i** sound in each word.

1. As a class, make a list of words that have the **short i** sound.

2. Use the Word Box, poem, and class list to make your list of Lesson Words.

3. In your notebook

- Print your Lesson Words.
- Circle the letter that makes the **short i** sound in each word.
- Add words to your Personal Dictionary.

Strategy Spot

Find a Rhyming Word

If you do not know how to spell a word, think of a word that rhymes with it. For example, **sit** rhymes with **hit**. Knowing how to spell **sit** can help you spell **hit**!

Zoom in on Your Words

1. **Sit-Hit** Write rhyming words for 3 Lesson Words. Underline letters that are the same in each pair of words.

2. **Be an Artist** Draw a picture of the boat in Shel Silverstein's poem.

3. **A to Z** Print each Lesson Word on a small piece of paper. Put your words in alphabetical order.

4. **Riddle Time** Find Word Box words that answer these riddles. Print the answers.

   a) I am large, pink, and can make lots of noise.

   b) You do this at school and at home.

   c) I am another word for **large**.

   d) I rhyme with **sit**, **bit**, and **lit**.

5. **Fancy Letters** Print 3 Lesson Words using fancy letters.

6. **At Home** Choose 3 Lesson Words. Use each word in a sentence.

FLASHBACK

Which strategy do you use to learn Lesson Words?

Graphs

Rinalda is going to have a birthday party. She asks her friends what they would like to eat.

Our Favourite Food

Cake is the favourite!

What flavour of cake do you think Rinalda should have at her party — chocolate, vanilla, or strawberry? Ask 5 friends what they think. Put their answers in a graph like Rinalda's. Give your graph a title!

---

6 SPELL CHECK

Patterns	Strategies
c, d, m, s d short a short e short i	1. Learn about spelling strategies 2. Draw a word picture 3. Use a dictionary 4. Look, cover, and write! 5. Find a rhyming word

Creating Your Word List

In your notebook

- List 8 words you need to practise.
- Look at letters you need to study.
- Circle these letters.
- These are your Review Lesson Words.

Zoom in on Your Words

1. **Word Pictures** Draw word pictures for 3 Lesson Words. Include them in your Personal Dictionary.

2. **Make Sentences** Choose 3 Lesson Words. Use each word in a sentence.

28

3. Missing Vowels Fill in the missing vowel to complete each word. Print the words in your notebook.

a) h _ t   **b)** t _ n   **c)** p _ g   **d)** b _ g

Try This! Make as many words as you can.

4. Picking Grapes Match letters to the **an** pattern. Print words you can make in your notebook.

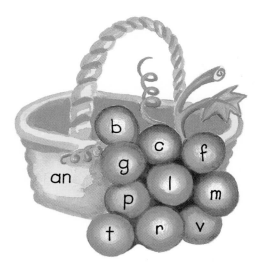

5. Bookmark Make a bookmark. Write words you like on your bookmark. Decorate it using coloured markers and crayons.

FLASHBACK

Look at the words you can spell. Congratulations, you are a super speller!

What would you eat at Tom's Place?

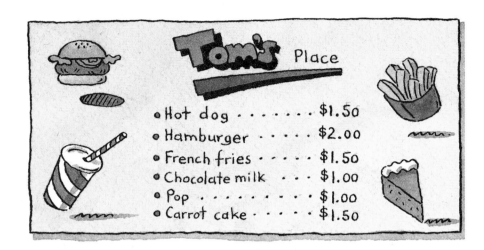

Word Box

log

come

hot

box

stop

gone

top

got

Creating Your Word List

Say these words:

come   hot   top

Listen for the **short o** sound. Is it the same in all the words?

1. As a class, make a list of words that have the **short o** sound.

30

2. Use the Word Box, menu, and class list to make your list of Lesson Words.

3. **In your notebook**
   - Print your Lesson Words.
   - Circle the letter that makes the **short o** sound in each word.
   - Add words to your Personal Dictionary.

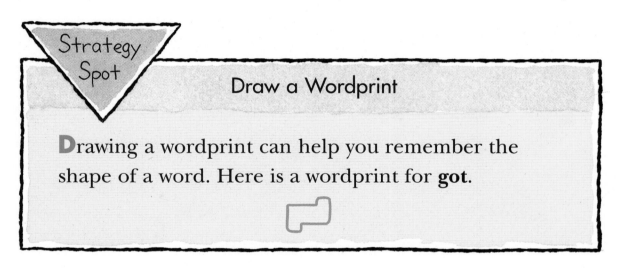

Strategy Spot

Draw a Wordprint

Drawing a wordprint can help you remember the shape of a word. Here is a wordprint for **got**.

Zoom in on Your Words

1. **Match Shapes to Words** Find Word Box words that match these wordprints.

Try This! Draw wordprints for 3 Lesson Words. Fill them in.

2. **Your Place** Make a menu for *your* restaurant. Circle words that have the **short o** sound.

3. **Missing o's** Add **o** to complete these Word Box words. Copy them in your notebook. Draw a picture of 1 word.
   a) b _ x   **b)** g _ ne   **c)** g _ t

4. **Find the Sound** Find the names of 4 things in this picture that have the **short o** sound.

 5. **At Home** Draw wordprints for the names of 3 family members.

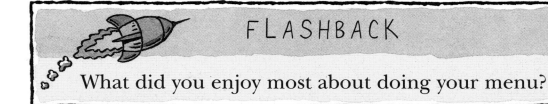

FLASHBACK

What did you enjoy most about doing your menu?

▶ FOCUS ON LANGUAGE
Vowels and Consonants

There are 26 letters in the alphabet. Some are vowels, but most are consonants.

Facts About Vowels	Facts About Consonants
• There are only 5 vowels – **a, e, i, o, u**. • Sometimes **y** can be a vowel (baby, cry). • Every word has at least 1 vowel. If it doesn't, it can't be a word!	• Most words contain more consonants than vowels. • Some consonants, like **x** and **z**, are not used often. • Some English words don't need a consonant to be a word (**a**, **I**).

1. Choose 5 words. Print the consonants. Leave a space for the vowels. Ask a partner to fill in the vowels.

2. Write each letter of the alphabet on a small piece of paper. Make words with 2 letters. Print them in your notebook. Now, try making bigger words.

What letter do you see in each sign?

Word Box

mud

run

jump

cut

fun

hut

tug

up

Creating Your Word List

Say these words:

mud   run   hut

Listen for the **short u** sound.

1. As a class, make a list of words that have the **short u** sound.

2. Use the Word Box, picture, and class list to make your list of Lesson Words.

3. In your notebook

- Print your Lesson Words.
- Circle the letter that makes the **short u** sound in each word.
- Add words to your Personal Dictionary.

Strategy Spot

Use Your Finger to Print

Using your finger as a pencil can help you to spell words. "Finger print" Lesson Words on your arm, a table, or a desk. Say each letter as you print it!

Zoom in on Your Words

1. Finger Printing Use the strategy to practise your Lesson Words.

2. Find the Treasure Help Chris find the treasure. On the next page, match each word to its clue.

| hut | run | mud | tug |

Dear Chris,
Follow these directions and you will find
the treasure.
1. _ _ _ through the park.
2. Do not step in the _ _ _ .
3. Look for the _ _ _ .
4. _ _ _ on the door to open it.

James

3. **Listen Carefully** Work with a partner.
Take turns saying the words. Print words
that have the **short u** sound.
   a) tube   **b)** cute   **c)** us   **d)** just
   e) cut   **f)** club   **g)** blue   **h)** hug

4. **At Home** Look at signs and street
names. Print words that have the
letter **u**. Circle words that have the
short u sound.

FLASHBACK

Which strategy is most helpful?

SOCIAL STUDIES

Self-Portrait

A self-portrait is a picture you draw of yourself. Look at Raj's self-portrait.

1. You are a special person. Draw a self-portrait.
2. Write a few sentences about what you like to do.

My name is Raj. I like to play hockey.

37

Can you answer this riddle?

I can be black or green. I am flat so people can write on me. I need to be cleaned each day. What am I?

Word Box

black

blue

clock

clown

flat

flag

glad

glass

Creating Your Word List

Say these words:

blue   clock   flat   glad

Listen to the sounds of the first 2 letters in each word. Now, say the words quickly. Hear how the first 2 letters "blend" together.

1. List words that have an **l blend**. Print your words in a chart like this one.

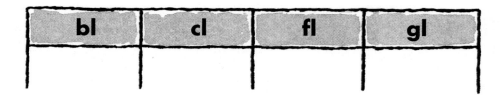

bl	cl	fl	gl

2. Use Word Box words, the riddle, and the chart to make your list of Lesson Words.

3. **In your notebook**
   - Print your Lesson Words.
   - Circle the **blend** in each word.
   - Add words to your Personal Dictionary.

Strategy Spot

Listen for Two Letters

In a blend, you hear both letters when you say the word slowly. When you say it quickly, the 2 letters blend to make a sound. That's why we call them blends.

Zoom in on Your Words

1. **Listen for Two Letters** Say your Lesson Words. Listen to the sounds of the 2 letters that make up each blend.

2. Word Meanings Print the Word Box word that

       a) is the opposite of **round**.
       b) is a colour (has 5 letters).
       c) is the same as **happy**.

3. Puzzle Pieces Match the blends and patterns to make words. Print them in your notebook.

4. Riddle Time Choose a Lesson Word. Make up a riddle for a partner to guess.

 5. At Home Make up a riddle. Ask a family member to guess your riddle.

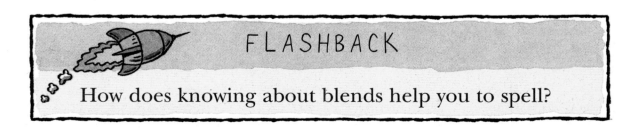

FLASHBACK

How does knowing about blends help you to spell?

FOCUS ON LANGUAGE
Types of Writing

There are many types of writing.

- invitations
- letters
- poems
- stories
- riddles
- posters

1. Choose 1 type of writing.

2. Make a rough copy of what you want to write. Check all the information.

3. Check for spelling errors. Ask a partner for help, or use a dictionary.

4. Make a good copy. Draw pictures to illustrate your work.

Read this poem. Talk with a partner about other things frogs like.

Frogs in Grass

Frogs in grass
Green grass, brown grass
Grass to leap in
Grass to sleep in
Green grass, brown grass
Frogs in grass

Word Box

bring

brother

brown

frog

from

green

grow

grass

Creating Your Word List

Say these words:

brown   frog   green

Listen to how the first letter blends with **r**. We call these **r-blend** words.

1. List words that have an **r blend**. Print your words in a chart like this one.

br	fr	gr

2. Use Word Box words and the chart to make your list of Lesson Words.

3. **In your notebook**
   - Print your Lesson Words.
   - Circle the **blend** in each word.
   - Add words to your Personal Dictionary.

Strategy Spot

Say It Right

Saying a word correctly helps you spell it correctly. Say 1 Lesson Word correctly. Listen to the letter sounds in the word.

Zoom in on Your Words

1. **Say It Right**   With a partner, take turns saying Word Box words. Say each word slowly. Did you say it correctly?

2. **Write Sentences**   Finish these sentences in your notebook.
   - **a)** I bring...
   - **b)** My brother...
   - **c)** I grow...

3. Making and Sorting Cards   Follow these steps to make cards.

a) Fold a piece of paper in half.

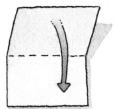

b) Fold it in half again 2 times.

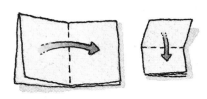

c) Open the paper. You should have 8 squares.

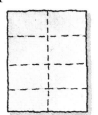

d) Cut along the folds.

Print a Lesson Word on each card. Put cards with the same blend in a pile. You should have 3 piles when you finish.

4. At Home   Ask family members to name their favourite colour. Print their answers. Underline colours that start with a blend.

FLASHBACK

How can a partner help you learn to spell?

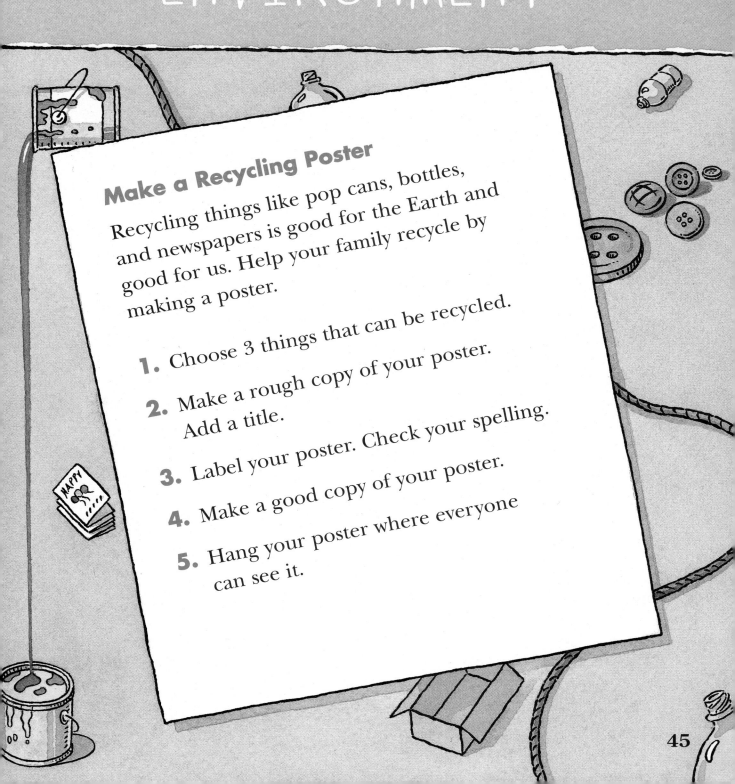

ENVIRONMENT

Make a Recycling Poster

Recycling things like pop cans, bottles, and newspapers is good for the Earth and good for us. Help your family recycle by making a poster.

1. Choose 3 things that can be recycled.

2. Make a rough copy of your poster. Add a title.

3. Label your poster. Check your spelling.

4. Make a good copy of your poster.

5. Hang your poster where everyone can see it.

Do you know other tongue twisters?

Small spoons spin in space.

Word Box

small

smart

spin

space

step

star

stay

just

Creating Your Word List

Say these words:

small   spin   stay

Listen to the sounds of the first 2 letters.
We call these **s-blend** words.

1. List words that have an **s blend**. Print your
words in a chart like this one.

sm	sp	st

2. Use Word Box words, the tongue twister, and the chart to make your list of Lesson Words.

3. **In your notebook**
   - Print your Lesson Words.
   - Circle the **blend** in each word.
   - Add words to your Personal Dictionary.

Learn Difficult Words

Follow these steps to learn difficult words.

1. Say each word aloud.

2. Print the word.

3. Circle letters that make the word hard to spell.

4. Print the word again.

Zoom in on Your Words

1. **Learn Difficult Words** Use the strategy to practise 5 Lesson Words.

2. **Wordprints** Make wordprints for 3 Lesson Words.

3. What's the Word? Match these words and pictures.

spin   spoon   smell   smile   star   space

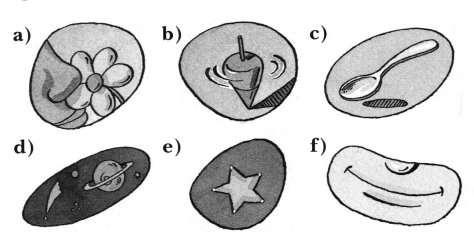

a)   b)   c)

d)   e)   f)

Did You Know?

The **st** blend can be at the beginning of a word (stay, start) and at the end of a word (just, best).

4. Make Sentences Choose 3 Lesson Words. Use each word in a sentence.

5. At Home Find **s-blend** words in a newspaper. Print your words in a chart like the one on page 46.

FLASHBACK

Tell a partner about your favourite spelling activity.

FOCUS ON LANGUAGE
Capital Letters

Capital letters are all around you. We use capital letters to spell
- a name (Benjy, Yasmin),
- place names (Alberta, Halifax),
- company names (Reebok, Nike),
- the first word in a sentence,
- the word, **I**.

1. Print your name and the names of 3 friends in your notebook. Print each capital letter in a different colour.

2. Print your address.

3. Add capital letters to these sentences. Print them in your notebook.
> **a)** i went to ottawa, ontario.
> **b)** amy and alexis are going to the zoo.
> **c)** mario and i are wearing reeboks.

Patterns	Strategies
short o short u bl, cl, fl, gl br, fr, gr sm, sp, st	1. Draw a wordprint 2. Use your finger to print 3. Listen for two letters 4. Say it right 5. Learn difficult words

Creating Your Word List

In your notebook

- List 8 words you need to practise.
- Look at letters you need to study.
- Circle these letters.
- These are your Review Lesson Words.

Zoom in on Your Words

1. **Say It Right** Work with a partner. Take turns saying Lesson Words. Ask your teacher for extra help.

2. **Wordprints** Draw wordprints for 3 Lesson Words. Include them in your Personal Dictionary.

3. Vowels and Consonants Print your Lesson Words in your notebook. (Circle) the vowels and underline the consonants.

<u>br</u>o<u>th</u>er

4. Can You Hear the Blend? Underline Lesson Words that have a blend.

5. Link Up Link words that rhyme. Print the pairs in your notebook.

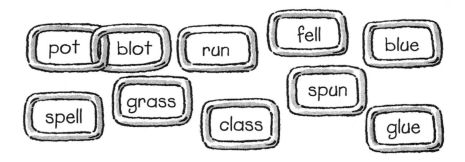

Try This! Add a rhyming word to each pair.

6. A to Z Write Lesson Words on pieces of paper. Put them in alphabetical order.

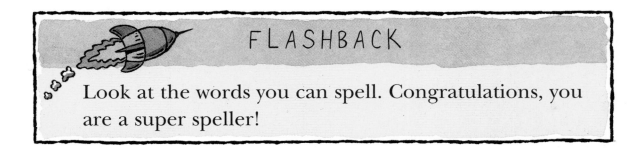

FLASHBACK

Look at the words you can spell. Congratulations, you are a super speller!

Have you had a day like this?

What a Day

What a day,
Oh what a day,
My baby brother ran away.
And now my tuba will not play.
I'm eight years old
and turning grey,
Oh what a day,
Oh what a day.

Shel Silverstein

Word Box

cake

came

gave

game

away

say

play

may

Creating Your Word List

Say these words:

cake   away   gave   may

Listen to the **long a** sound in each word.

1. List words that have the **long a** sound
   in a chart like the one on the next page.

a + e	ay	other

2. Use Word Box words, the poem, and the chart to make your list of Lesson Words.

3. In your notebook
  - Print your Lesson Words.
  - Circle letter(s) that make the **long a** sound in each word.
  - Add words to your Personal Dictionary.

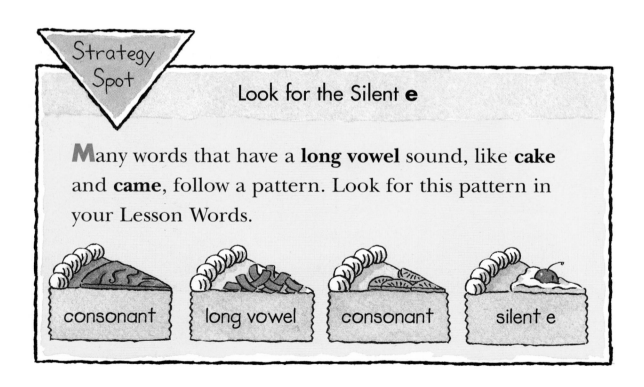

Strategy Spot

Look for the Silent **e**

Many words that have a **long vowel** sound, like **cake** and **came**, follow a pattern. Look for this pattern in your Lesson Words.

consonant   long vowel   consonant   silent e

Zoom in on Your Words

1. **An Adding Machine** Put words in the machine. Add an **e** and say the words. How does the sound change?

at
tap
cap
can

2. **Sentence Starters** Complete these sentences in your notebook.
   a) The cake ... **b)** I like to play ...

3. **Wordprints** Make wordprints for 3 Lesson Words.

4. **At Home** Choose a page from a book. Count words that have the **long a** sound.

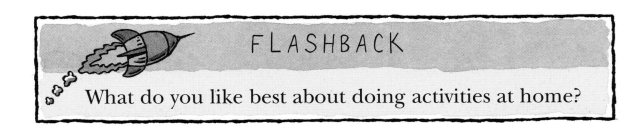

FLASHBACK

What do you like best about doing activities at home?

54

HOME

Recipes

A recipe tells you how to make something. You can find recipes in cookbooks and magazines. Here is Shane's recipe for making grape popsicles.

Shane's Greatly Grape Popsicles

Ingredients
1 ice cube tray
¼ bottle grape juice
12 toothpicks
1 sheet plastic wrap

Steps
1. Pour the grape juice into the tray
2. Place plastic wrap tightly around the tray
3. Put a toothpick into the centre of each cube
4. Put the tray in the freezer for 3 hours

Serving Size
Makes 12 popsicles

1. What is your favourite food?
2. Find a recipe for it in a cookbook, or ask someone at home.
3. Print its title on a piece of paper.

The bird must use words with the **long e** sound to make its nest. How many words can it use?

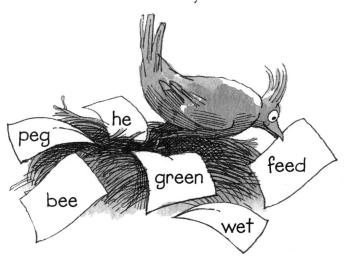

Creating Your Word List

Word Box

feed

each

read

seat

tree

week

eat

free

Say these words:

Listen to the **long e** sound in each word.

1. List words that have the **long e** sound in a chart like this one.

ee	ea	other

2. Use Word Box words, the picture, and the chart to make your list of Lesson Words.

3. In your notebook
- Print your Lesson Words.
- Circle letters that make the **long e** sound in each word.
- Add words to your Personal Dictionary.

Strategy Spot

Keep a List of Words

Words like **the** and **a** are used often. To remember how to spell these words:
- print them in your Personal Dictionary,
- add them to your class word bag or word wall.

Zoom in on Your Words

1. Everyday Words Write 5 words that you use often. Trade lists with a partner. Did you write the same words? Add new words to your Personal Dictionary.

2. **Word Groups**   Find the Word Box word that completes each sentence. Print the words in your notebook.

        a) Seven days make a _ _ _ _.

        b) _ _ _ _ book is red.

        c) The _ _ _ _ grew by the river.

        d) I like to _ _ _ ice cream.

3. **Fancy Letters**   Print (or write) 3 Lesson Words using fancy letters.

dream

4. **Read, Books, Enjoy**   Say a Lesson Word. Your partner says a word it makes him or her think of. Print the words. How many words can you say and print in 1 minute?

5. **At Home**   Play the word game with a family member.

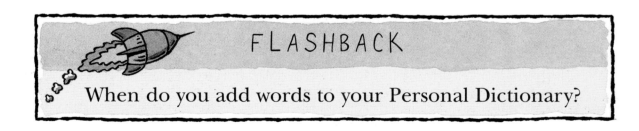

FLASHBACK

When do you add words to your Personal Dictionary?

▷ FOCUS ON LANGUAGE
Periods

Sentences can end with a period (.), a question mark (?), or an exclamation mark (!). Most sentences end with a period.

1. Choose a story from your writing folder. Read the story and find the periods. How many periods did you find?

2. The story below has no periods. Copy it in your notebook. Add periods. (Hint: The story needs 5 periods.)

Alex's cat, Pumpkin, was sleeping Suddenly, a squirrel ran past her Pumpkin woke She started to chase the squirrel As she ran, she knocked over a glass of water that was beside Alex's new book Alex was not happy!

Imagine that you are a reporter for YTNN News. This report has just come in. Read it aloud.

This just in...Nine ducks and five hens have escaped from Ike's farm! If you see them please contact YTNN! We must find them—they might bite!

Word Box

five
like
fine
nine
ride
time
kind
find

Creating Your Word List

Say these words:

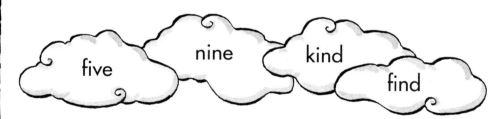

five   nine   kind   find

Listen to the **long i** sound in each word.

1. List words that have the **long i** sound in a chart like this one.

i + e	ind

2. Use Word Box words, the picture, and the chart to make your list of Lesson Words.

3. **In your notebook**
   - Print your Lesson Words.
   - Circle letter(s) that make the **long i** sound in each word.
   - Add words to your Personal Dictionary.

Strategy Spot

Make a Word Wall

A word wall can help you spell. On cards, print words you need to learn to spell. Your teacher can put them on the wall.

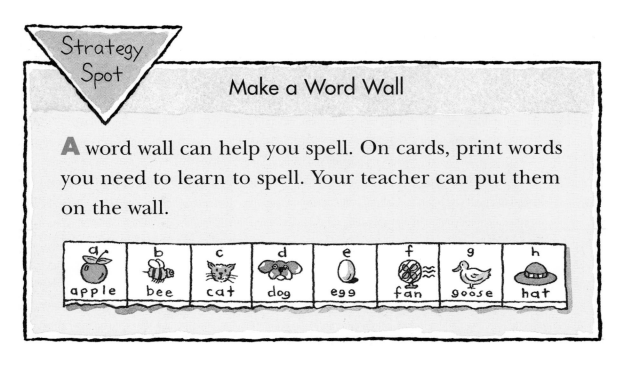

Zoom in on Your Words

1. **Words for a Wall** Print 3 Lesson Words on cards. Check your spelling in a dictionary, or ask a partner for help. Your teacher can add your cards to the word wall.

2. Dear Alex In your notebook, print Word Box words that complete these sentences.

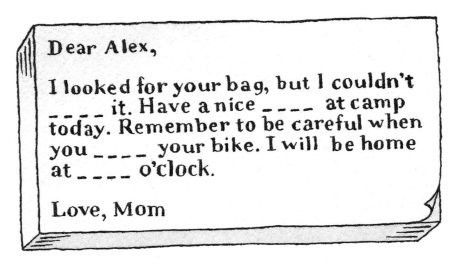

Dear Alex,

I looked for your bag, but I couldn't
_ _ _ _ it. Have a nice _ _ _ _ at camp
today. Remember to be careful when
you _ _ _ _ your bike. I will be home
at _ _ _ _ o'clock.

Love, Mom

3. Station Name
Every letter in
YTNN stands for
a word. Make up
a name for *your*
television station.

Young
Television
News
Network

4. At Home Write about your day.
Circle words that have **long vowel**
sounds.

FLASHBACK

How does the word wall help you when you write?

Connecting with
LITERATURE

Picture Books

Libraries have many kinds of books:

dictionaries

textbooks

chapter books

cookbooks

novels

picture books

THE VERY
HUNGRY
CATERPILLAR
by Eric Carle

Picture books are fun to read because they have lots
of illustrations (drawings). Tamelle's favourite book is
The Very Hungry Caterpillar. It is written *and* illustrated
by Eric Carle.

1. In your notebook, print the name of your favourite book.

2. Print the name of the book's author and illustrator.

3. Talk about why you like the book with a partner.

4. Read it to your partner.

Long o

Find the names of 4 things in this picture that have the **long o** sound.

Word Box

home

boat

go

coat

no

most

so

old

Creating Your Word List

Say these words:

home   boat   most   old

Listen to the **long o** sound in each word.

1. List words that have the **long o** sound in a chart like this one.

o + e	oa	o

2. Use Word Box words, the picture, and the chart to make your list of Lesson Words.

3. **In your notebook**
   - Print your Lesson Words.
   - Circle letter(s) that make the **long o** sound in each word.
   - Add words to your Personal Dictionary.

Say a Word Slowly

Saying a word slowly can help you spell it. Listen for letter sounds.

Zoom in on Your Words

1. **Say It Slowly** Use the strategy to practise spelling your Lesson Words.

2. **Wordprints** Choose 5 Lesson Words. Make a wordprint for each word, then fill in the letters.

3. Word Groups
Find the Word Box word that completes each sentence. Print the words in your notebook.

a) Her _ _ _ _ has no buttons.
b) How _ _ _ is he?
c) The _ _ _ _ was in the water.
d) _ _ _ _ of the people went to class.
e) She went _ _ _ _ after school.

4. One-Word Poem
Work with a partner. Say the word, **go**. Your partner says the word differently. Take turns saying the word. Change the way you say it each time.

Try This! Use another word that has the **long o** sound to make a 1-word poem.

5. At Home
Choose 3 Lesson Words. Use each word in a sentence.

FLASHBACK

What did you like best about this lesson?

FOCUS ON LANGUAGE
Question Marks

When a sentence asks a question, it ends with a question mark (?). Read these 2 sentences. Print the sentence that asks a question in your notebook.

I like to ride my bike.
Do you like to ride your bike?

1. Unscramble these sentences. Print them in your notebook.
   a) name? What is your
   b) What to bed? time you do go
   c) old you? are How
   d) your is Where coat?

2. In your notebook, print 3 questions you would like to ask your favourite author.

Read the sentences. Are all the sentences true?

1. Bears are huge.
2. Monkeys can use cups to drink.
3. Bugs are cute.
4. Whales can be blue.

Word Box

cute
use
June
true
you
rule
huge
few

Creating Your Word List

Say these words:

Listen to the **long u** sound in each word.

1. List words that have the **long u** sound in a chart like this one.

u + e	u	other

2. Use Word Box words, the sentences, and the chart to make your list of Lesson Words.

3. **In your notebook**
   - Print your Lesson Words.
   - Circle letter(s) that make the **long u** sound in each word.
   - Add words to your Personal Dictionary.

Read Aloud to Proofread

Read aloud your work to find spelling and punctuation mistakes. As you read, circle your mistakes. When you are finished reading, go back and correct your work.

Zoom in on Your Words

1. **Proofread Your Work** Use the strategy to proofread a story you have written.

   Try This! Ask a partner to proofread your work. Did she or he find other mistakes?

2. Choose Carefully! Say the words on the apple tree. In your notebook, print *only* the words that have the **long u** sound.

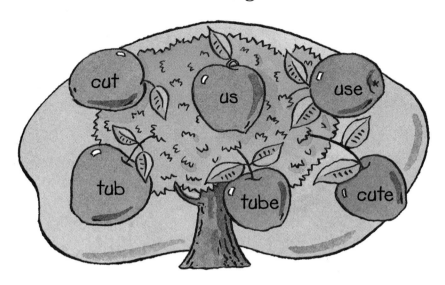

3. Fill in the Blanks In your notebook, print Word Box words that complete these sentences.

     a) Please _ _ _ a pencil.

     b) School is finished in _ _ _ _ .

     c) Is it _ _ _ _ you're moving?

 4. At Home In a book, find 5 words that have the **long u** sound. Print them in your notebook.

FLASHBACK

How does reading aloud help you find mistakes?

70

MATH

Other Ways to Measure

Measuring things can be lots of fun! You do not always have to measure them with a ruler. You can use your fingers, hands, or feet to measure something. Jose used his hand to measure the length of his desk.

1 desk = 6 hands

1. Find 3 things in your classroom you would like to measure. Use your fingers, hands, or feet to measure their length.

2. Print your answers in a chart like this:

Object	Length

3. Measure something else the same way.

71

Patterns	Strategies
long a	1. Look for the silent e
long e	2. Keep a list of words
long i	3. Make a word wall
long o	4. Say a word slowly
long u	5. Read aloud to proofread

Creating Your Word List

In your notebook

- List 8 words you need to practise.
- Look at letters you need to study.
- Circle these letters.
- These are your Review Lesson Words.

Zoom in on Your Words

1. **Say a Word Slowly** Choose 5 Lesson Words. Say each word slowly.

2. **Make Sentences** Choose 3 Lesson Words. Use each word in a sentence.

3. Spin the Wheel
Spin the wheel to make words. Print the words in your notebook.

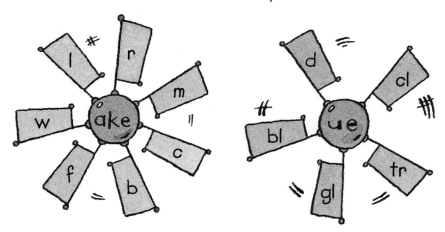

4. Help the Cars Move
Cars that have a **long vowel** sound must follow the sign. Print the cars that should follow the sign.

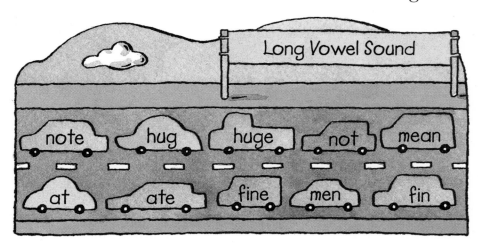

FLASHBACK

Look at the words you can spell. Congratulations, you are a super speller!

73

Read this funny poem to a partner.

Be Prepared

Slippery
Sloppery
Slushery snow
Do up your snowshoes
And let's go.

Drippery
Droppery
Drizzery rain
Open your "yella" umbrella
Again.

Mistery
Moistery
Mustery fog
Make sure you have
A strong leash for your dog.

Sonja Dunn

Creating Your Word List

Say these words:

baby   city   cry   fly

Word Box

party

my

story

try

baby

cry

city

fly

74

Listen to the sound the letter **y** makes in the words in the clouds. What sounds can **y** make?

1. List words that have **y** as a vowel in a chart like this one.

y (long e sound)	y (long i sound)

2. Use Word Box words and the chart to make your list of Lesson Words.

3. **In your notebook**
   - Print your Lesson Words.
   - Circle **y** as a vowel in each word. Print the sound **y** makes (**long e** or **long i**) beside each word.
   - Add words to your Personal Dictionary.

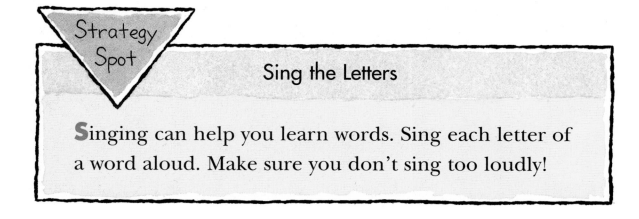

Strategy Spot

Sing the Letters

Singing can help you learn words. Sing each letter of a word aloud. Make sure you don't sing too loudly!

Zoom in on Your Words

1. Sing the Letters   Choose 5 Lesson
Words. Sing their letters.

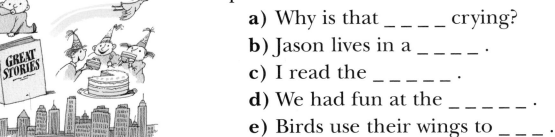

2. Use the Picture Clues   Use the clues to
complete these sentences.

      a) Why is that _ _ _ _ crying?
      b) Jason lives in a _ _ _ _ .
      c) I read the _ _ _ _ _ .
      d) We had fun at the _ _ _ _ _ .
      e) Birds use their wings to _ _ _ .

3. What's the Sound?   Copy these words
in your notebook. Circle words that end
with the **long e** sound. Underline words
that end with the **long i** sound.

    a) cry   **b)** party   **c)** try   **d)** baby

4. At Home   Names like **Jenny** end
in **y**. Ask a family member to help
you list names that end in **y**.

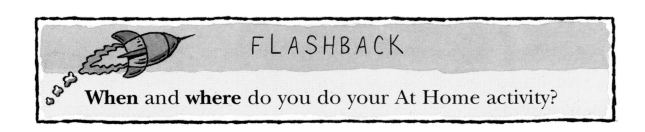

FLASHBACK

When and **where** do you do your At Home activity?

FOCUS ON LANGUAGE
Getting Ideas for Writing

Even famous authors get their ideas from somewhere! Look for ideas in places like these.

1. Make a list of writing ideas.

2. Cut out magazine and newspaper pictures. Add them to your writing folder.

3. Keep adding ideas to your list.

4. Use your list the next time you write a story.

Paulo, Sheetal, and Anna are running a race. Who will finish first?

Word Box

adding

jumping

running

going

hopping

doing

eating

helping

Creating Your Word List

Say these words:

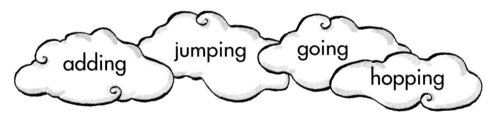

These words are the same in 2 ways. They are action words and they end in **-ing**.

1. As a class, make a list of words that end in **-ing**.

2. Use the Word Box, picture, and class list to make your list of Lesson Words.

3. In your notebook

- Print your Lesson Words.
- Circle the **-ing** ending in each word.
- Add words to your Personal Dictionary.

Strategy Spot

Look for the Root Word

The **root** is the main part of a word. Knowing the root of a word can help you spell it (walking – walk).

Zoom in on Your Words

1. Work with Roots Stop the balloons from flying away! Add **-ing** to the roots. Print the words you make.

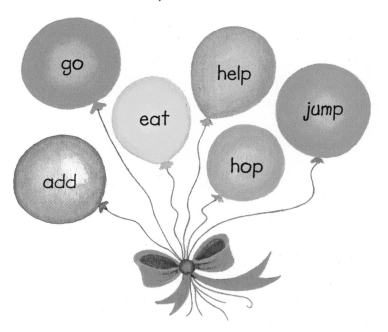

go

help

eat

jump

hop

add

2. **Run + n + ing** Some words double the last consonant when **-ing** is added. Find the 2 Word Box words where this happens.

3. **Act It Out** Choose 1 Word Box word. Act it out for your partner. Your partner guesses your word. Take turns.

4. **Go, Going, Gone** Print the Word Box word that completes each group.
   a) add, _ _ _ _ _ _, added
   b) hop, _ _ _ _ _ _ _, hopped
   c) do, _ _ _ _ _, done
   d) eat, _ _ _ _ _ _, ate

5. **At Home** List things you do at home, like washing and reading, that end in **-ing**. Share your list with a family member.

FLASHBACK

What do you have to remember when you add **-ing** to some words?

80

FOCUS ON LANGUAGE
Verbs

Think of things you do every day, like reading. These action words are called **verbs**.

1. Look at these pictures. Print the verbs in your notebook.

2. Make a list of 10 verbs you do.

3. Choose 2 verbs. Write a sentence for each. Circle the verbs.

Say or sing this chant softly.

My mother wanted peaches,
My brother wanted pears,
My father wanted fifty cents,
To fix the broken stairs.

My mother ate the peaches,
My brother ate the pears,
My father ate the fifty cents,
And fell right down the stairs.

Word Box

mother
father
letter
dinner
after
grandfather
grandmother
teacher

Creating Your Word List

Say these words:

mother   father   letter   dinner

Listen to the sound **er** makes in each word.

1. As a class, make a list of **er** words.

2. Use Word Box words and the class list
to make your list of Lesson Words.

3. **In your notebook**
   - Print your Lesson Words.
   - Circle **er** in each word.
   - Add words to your Personal Dictionary.

Strategy Spot

Give It a Go!

When you don't know how to spell a word, give it a go! Leave blank spaces for parts you can't spell. Finish writing, then check your word in a dictionary.

Zoom in on Your Words

1. **Give It a Go**   Use the strategy to practise your Lesson Words.

2. **Use the Clues!**   Print Word Box words that answer these clues.

   a) your mother's father, your

   _ _ _ _ _ _ _ _ _ _

   b) something that you write,

   a _ _ _ _ _ _

   c) someone in your class, your

   _ _ _ _ _ _ _

3. **New Words** Adding **er** to some root words makes new words. Print words the **er** machine can make.

teach
farm
great
kind
small

4. **Build a Pyramid** Choose a Lesson Word. Print the first letter at the top. Next, print 2 letters. Continue until you have printed all the letters.

Try This! Make word pyramids for 2 other Lesson Words.

m
mo
mot
moth
mothe
mother

5. **At Home** Maybe you want to be a teacher when you grow up. List jobs that you think you would enjoy.

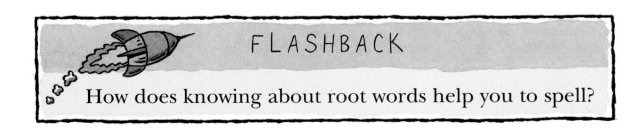

FLASHBACK

How does knowing about root words help you to spell?

MUSIC

Make a Chant

Do you know this chant?

> One, two, three, four,
> Mary at the cottage door.
> Five, six, seven, eight,
> Eating cherries off a plate.
> O-U-T spells out!

Listen to Marcello's version of the same chant:

> One, two, three, four,
> Mommy's calling at the door.
> Five, six, seven, eight,
> Better go before you're late.
> O-U-T spells out!

Make your own version of this chant!

1. Copy line 1.
2. Pick a word that rhymes with **four**. Your second line will end with this word.
3. Copy line 3.
4. Pick a word that rhymes with **eight**. Your fourth line will end with this word.
5. Copy the last line.
6. Read your chant to your classmates!

The names of 5 things in the picture begin with **sh**. Can you find them?

Word Box

she

fish

ship

wish

shirt

wash

shell

push

Creating Your Word List

Say these words:

she   shirt   fish   push

Listen to the sound **sh** makes in each word. Does it sound the same in all of the words?

1. List words that have **sh** in a chart like the one on the next page.

sh- (beginning)	-sh (end)

2. Use Word Box words, the picture, and the chart to make your list of Lesson Words.

3. In your notebook
- Print your Lesson Words.
- Circle **sh** in each word.
- Add words to your Personal Dictionary.

Does It Look Right?

When you are not sure how to spell a word, write it 2 ways. Choose the way that looks right. Which of these words looks right?

fisshing   fishing

Zoom in on Your Words

1. Choose the Word Use the strategy to practise your Lesson Words.

2. What's the Word? Look at the pictures. Find rhyming Word Box words. Print them in your notebook.

3. Scrunched-up Words Three Word Box words have been scrunched together. Print them in your notebook.

shipshirtpush

4. Word Pictures Draw word pictures for 3 Lesson Words.

5. At Home Print rhyming words for 2 Lesson Words. Draw a picture of the words.

FLASHBACK

How does the Strategy Spot help you to spell your Lesson Words?

Magazine Covers

Magazines are everywhere! You can find them in libraries, stores, and at home! Their covers tell you what they are about and what is inside.

This is an example of a magazine for kids.

1. Look at a magazine in the library or at home. Use a chart like this to list important information on the cover.

Title	Price	Headline	Information

2. Design your own magazine cover. Share it with a partner.

How fast can you say this tongue twister?

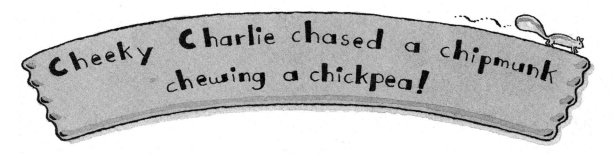

Cheeky Charlie chased a chipmunk chewing a chickpea!

Word Box

chin

such

chop

chip

much

child

peach

children

Creating Your Word List

Say these words:

chin

chop

such

peach

Listen to the sound **ch** makes in each word. Does it sound the same in all of the words?

1. List words that have **ch** in a chart like this one.

ch- (beginning)	-ch (end)

2. Use the Word Box, tongue twister, and chart to make your list of Lesson Words.

3. **In your notebook**
   - Print your Lesson Words.
   - Circle **ch** in each word.
   - Add words to your Personal Dictionary.

Strategy Spot

Use Your Personal Dictionary

Check your Personal Dictionary when you need to spell a word you don't know. You may have written it in your dictionary. *Add* words you want to learn how to spell.

Zoom in on Your Words

1. **New Words** Add 3 words you want to practise to your Personal Dictionary.

2. **Twist Your Tongue** Add actions to a favourite tongue twister, like this one.

Sally sells seashells down by the seashore.

3. Help the Chugs Add **ch** to each chug bug to make a word.

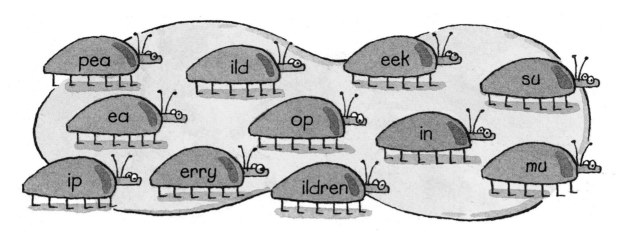

pea

ild

eek

su

ea

op

in

mu

ip

erry

ildren

4. Bumblebee Play this game with a partner.

   a) Player A chooses a Lesson Word and makes a dash for each letter.

   b) Player B guesses a letter at a time.

   c) For each wrong guess, Player A draws a part of the bumblebee.

   d) Only one guess of the whole word is allowed.

 5. At Home List food names, like **peach**, that contain **ch**.

FLASHBACK

How would you help a friend learn Lesson Words?

FOCUS ON ART
Draw a Picture Before You Write

When you have a story idea, it helps to draw pictures first. Then you can write sentences to go with each picture. Here is how to write a picture story.

1. Make 4 boxes.

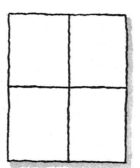

2. Number the boxes 1 to 4.

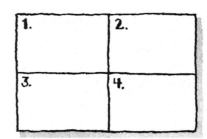

3. Draw a picture in each box.

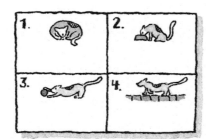

4. Write a sentence that tells about each picture.

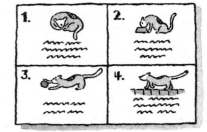

Patterns	Strategies
y as a vowel -ing er sh ch	1. Sing the letters 2. Look for the root word 3. Give it a go! 4. Does it look right? 5. Use your Personal Dictionary

Creating Your Word List

In your notebook

- List 8 words you need to practise.
- Look at letters you need to study.
- Circle these letters.
- These are your Review Lesson Words.

Zoom in on Your Words

1. Does It Look Right? Trade Lesson Word lists with a partner. Your partner chooses 1 of your words and prints it 2 ways. Choose the way that looks right, then check your choice. Take turns.

2. **Colourful!** Print your Lesson Words. Leave a space between each letter. Use 1 colour to trace over letters that make the word hard to spell. Trace over the other letters using another colour.

3. **Make Sentences** Choose 3 Lesson Words. Use each word in a sentence.

4. **Jumping** Underline Lesson Words that are verbs.

5. **Make New Words** Make new words by adding **-ing** or **er** (or both) to these root words.

teach
work
sing
hurt
run
great

FLASHBACK

Look at the words you can spell. Congratulations, you are a super speller!

Read this poem silently.

Secrets

Some things are for telling
Some things are for yelling
Some things are for whispering
To flowers or the sky
Other secrets wing their way
To light by and by

Sheree Fitch

Word Box

that
the
them
then
there
they
with
both

Creating Your Word List

Say these words:

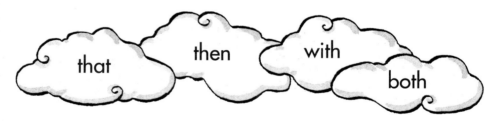

that then with both

Listen to the sound of **th** in each word.

1. List **th** words in a chart like this one.

th- (beginning)	-th (end)

2. Use Word Box words, the poem, and the chart to make your list of Lesson Words.

3. **In your notebook**
   - Print your Lesson Words.
   - Circle **th** in each word.
   - Add words to your Personal Dictionary.

Strategy Spot

Ask a Partner to Proofread

Ask a partner to proofread a story or poem you have written. Often, they can see mistakes more easily.

Zoom in on Your Words

1. **Sharing Writing** Give a story you have written to a partner. Did your partner find other mistakes?

2. **Scrunched-up Words** Three Word Box words have been scrunched together. Find them and print them in your notebook.

thatthenboth

Try This! Print 3 Lesson Words. Ask a partner to find your words.

3. What's Your Word? Whisper a Lesson Word to a partner. Your partner whispers a word it makes him or her think of.

4. The th Rabbit The rabbit must make **th** words before he can eat the carrots. In your notebook, print the words he can make.

5. Find the Word Print the Word Box word that fits each group of words.

       a) now and _ _ _ _
       b) here, _ _ _ _ _ , everywhere
       c) me, she, he, _ _ _ _

 6. At Home List places and times where you *must* whisper.

FLASHBACK

How did you help your partner proofread?

98

FOCUS ON LANGUAGE
Reading for Meaning

When you proofread, you check spelling, punctuation, capital letters, *and* meaning. Ask yourself these questions:

> Does my story make sense?
> Did I write what I wanted to say?

1. Read a story you have written. Ask yourself these questions. If you answer "no," rewrite your story.

2. Read this story. With a partner, decide how you would change it. Print the story, with your changes, in your notebook.

Alanna, Michael, and Sydney decided to go to the park yesterday. They thought they were going to have so much fun! The dog was barking. The ice cream store was closed. They had ice cream at home.

Bark, Bark

Double Consonants

Read this news headline to your partner.

Word Box

ball
bell
fill
call
will
hill
miss
class

Creating Your Word List

Say these words:

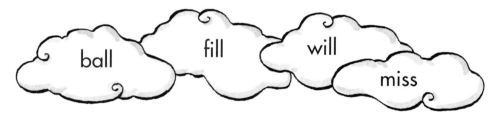

Look at the last 2 consonants in each word.
Did you notice that they are double (2)?
What sounds do they make?

1. List words that have **double consonants**
in a chart like this one.

ll	ss

2. Use Word Box words, the headline, and the chart to make your list of Lesson Words.

3. In your notebook
- Print your Lesson Words.
- Circle the **double consonant** in each word.
- Add words to your Personal Dictionary.

Strategy Spot

List Words with the Same Pattern

Words with the same sound can have the same spelling. Knowing patterns that make these sounds will help you learn new words. For example, if you know how to spell **bell**, it will be easier to spell **tell**.

Zoom in on Your Words

1. Word Web Choose a Word Box word that ends in **ll**. Make a word web like this one.

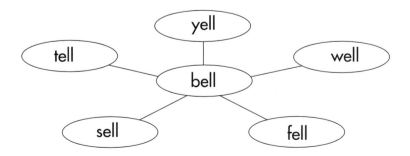

2. A Letter Machine
Change the first letter of these words to make Word Box words. Print each pair of words in your notebook.

tall
fell
bill
kiss

3. Sentence Starters
Complete these sentences in your notebook.

a) I miss...   **b)** The bell...   **c)** Call...

4. At Home
Make a collage of words from newspapers or magazines that end in a double final consonant.

FLASHBACK

What did you like best about making a collage?

FOCUS ON LANGUAGE
Compound Words

Words like **classroom** are called **compound** words. They are made up of 2 smaller words. A compound has the same meaning as the 2 small words.

class **+** room **=** classroom

1. Print these words in your notebook. Draw a line between 2 words to make a compound word. The first 1 has been done for you.

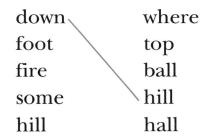

down	where
foot	top
fire	ball
some	hill
hill	hall

2. Work with a partner. List other compound words. Make a class list of compound words.

3. Choose 1 compound word. Draw a picture of your word.

Read this riddle. Can you guess the answer?

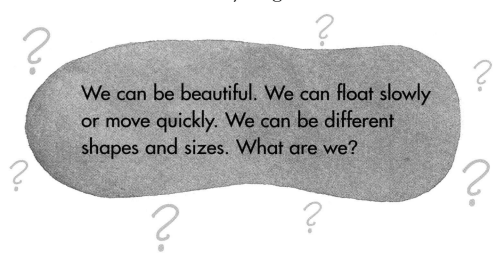

We can be beautiful. We can float slowly or move quickly. We can be different shapes and sizes. What are we?

Word Box

beds

cakes

dogs

hats

homes

letters

rules

teachers

Creating Your Word List

Say these words:

cakes   hats   letters   teachers

What is the same about each word? These words are plurals – they mean more than 1 (**1** home, **2** home**s**).

1. As a class, make a list of plural words.

2. Use the Word Box, riddle, and class list to make your list of Lesson Words.

3. **In your notebook**
   - Print your Lesson Words.
   - Circle the final **s** in each word.
   - Add words to your Personal Dictionary.

Strategy Spot

Sound Out Each Letter in a Word

Sounding out each letter in a word can help you spell it. Sound all the letters in a plural. Listen for the sound of **s** at the end of the word.

sssss

Zoom in on Your Words

1. **Sounding Out** Sound out letters in 5 Lesson Words. Did you hear each letter? Print the words in your notebook.

2. Colourful Words Print each Lesson Word on a piece of paper. Leave a space between each letter. Trace **s** in one colour. Trace other letters in another colour.

3. Sentence Starters Complete these sentence starters in your notebook.
a) The dogs...   **b)** Cakes are...
c) Teachers...   **d)** We wear hats...

4. Use the Letters Print each letter in **teacher** on a small piece of paper. Use the letters to make new words. How many words can you make using these letters?

t   e   a   c   h   e   r

5. At Home Choose 3 Lesson Words. Draw word pictures for each word.

FLASHBACK

What was your favourite activity in this lesson?

FOCUS ON LANGUAGE
Nouns

Nouns are words that name people, animals, places, and things. Look at the Word Box on page 104. Each word is a noun.

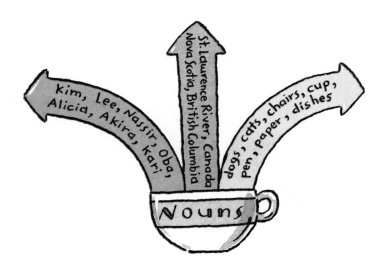

1. Find the nouns in these sentences.
   a) The bird ate its food.
   b) Ottawa is a pretty city.
   c) Amir lives on Dennie Street.
   d) The hill was large.
   e) Bob is a brown cat.

2. Look around your classroom. Print the names of 5 nouns. Trade lists with a partner. Together, make a list of 10 nouns.

The Beavers didn't think real beavers played hockey, then Woody joined the team.

Word Box

can't

don't

I'm

didn't

he's

I've

she's

we've

Creating Your Word List

Say these words:

don't   I'm   she's   I've

Each word is a **contraction** – 2 words are put together to make a new word. The apostrophe (') takes the place of some letters.

1. As a class, make a list of contractions.

2. Use Word Box words and the class list to make your list of Lesson Words.

3. **In your notebook**
   - Print your Lesson Words.
   - Add words to your Personal Dictionary.

Make a Foldover

Making foldovers is a fun way to learn new words.

1. Copy a word on the bottom half of a small piece of paper.

2. Fold the top half of the paper over the word.

3. Print your word on top without peeking!

4. Open the paper and check your spelling.

Zoom in on Your Words

1. Fold It Over Choose 3 Lesson Words. Make a foldover for each word.

2. **Matching Words** Copy these words in your notebook. Draw lines to match each contraction with the words that make it up.

can't	she is
don't	did not
she's	he is
I'm	can not
didn't	I have
he's	I am
I've	do not

3. **Print a Contraction** Look at these pictures. Choose 1 object. Write a sentence about it that has a contraction.

4. **At Home** Find 3 contractions in a newspaper or magazine. Print them in your notebook.

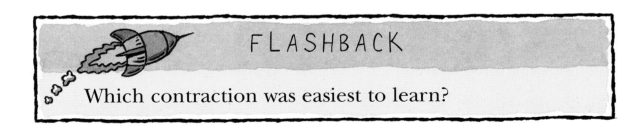

FLASHBACK

Which contraction was easiest to learn?

Advertising

Advertisements try to get your attention. A good ad will make you want to buy something. Here's an ad for bicycles.

When you're ready to ride,
Hill bikes are ready for you!

1. Would you buy a Hill bicycle? Talk about the ad with a partner. Decide if it is a good advertisement.

2. Turn this advertisement into a television ad. Act it out with a partner.

Read this poem to a partner.

As Far

As far as
the eye
can see
and as
far as
the sea
can eye
there will
always be
a sky

George Swede

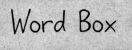

Word Box

buy

by

one

won

eye

I

see

sea

Creating Your Word List

Say these words:

These words are **homophones**. They sound the same, but have different spellings.

1. As a class, make a list of homophones. Print the meaning of each word or draw a picture in a chart like this one.

Homophone Pairs	

2. Use Word Box words and the class list to make your list of Lesson Words.

3. **In your notebook**
   - Print your Lesson Words.
   - Sound out each word.
   - Add words to your Personal Dictionary.

Strategy Spot

Highlight Words in Your List

When you print your Lesson Words, underline words that need extra attention. Use favourite spelling strategies to learn these words.

Zoom in on Your Words

1. **Highlight Words** Print your Lesson Words. Underline words that need extra attention. Choose strategies to help you learn these words.

2. **I See the Sea** Use Word Box words to complete the sentences. Print the words in your notebook.
   a) _ like your blue _ _ _ s.
   b) I can _ _ _ the _ _ _ from my window.
   c) She _ _ _ a trip for _ _ _ person.
   d) He walked _ _ the coat he wanted to _ _ _.

3. **As Far as the Eye Can See** Look out the window. How far can you see? Draw a picture of what you see.

4. **At Home** Use 2 homophones in a sentence.

FLASHBACK
What was the most difficult thing to learn in this lesson?

114

Shape Poems

Make a shape poem by printing the words in a certain shape.
Do you see how these words make the shape of a snake?

Sneaking, slithering, sliding through the grass

1. Choose an object.

2. Write a simple poem about the object.

3. Print your poem in the shape of this object.

Patterns	Strategies
th double consonants plurals contractions homophones	1. Ask a partner to proofread 2. List words with the same pattern 3. Sound out each letter in a word 4. Make a foldover 5. Highlight words in your list

Creating Your Word List

In your notebook

- List 8 words you need to practise.
- Look at letters you need to study.
- Circle these letters.
- These are your Review Lesson Words.

Zoom in on Your Words

1. List Words Print Lesson Words that have the same pattern beside each other.

there both class letters

2. Sound Out Your Words Sound out each letter in a Lesson Word. Print the word without looking at it. Check your spelling. Do the same with other words.

3. Put Words Together Match the word parts. Print the words you make in your notebook.

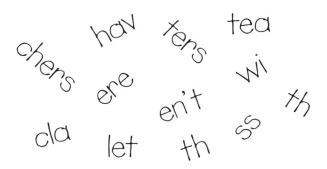

4. Sort Your Words Print each Lesson Word on a piece of paper. Sort your words different ways – by beginning or end letters, by meaning, and by number of letters.

5. Make a Foldover Practise your Lesson Words by making a foldover.

FLASHBACK

Look at the words you can spell. Congratulations, you are a super speller!

Enjoy this poem!

The Sun's Behind the Houses

The sun's behind the houses.
   The streetlights glow.
Hiding in the hedges,
   I know it's time to go.
I know the game is over.
   The kids all say goodnight
      But just a little longer,
      I stay a little longer,
watching in the autumn chill
the closing golden light.

Loris Lesynski

Creating Your Word List

Say these words:

make   little   drum   street

Name the vowel sounds you hear.

Word Box

about

over

tube

went

little

make

night

long

drum

street

---

1. As a class, make a list of words. Circle vowel sound(s) in each word.

2. Use the Word Box, poem, and class list to make your list of Lesson Words.

3. **In your notebook**
   - Print your Lesson Words.
   - Circle the **vowel sound(s)** in each word.
   - Add words to your Personal Dictionary.

Strategy Spot

Hear How Some Vowel Patterns Make the Same Sound

Some **vowel patterns**, like **ue** (true) and **ew** (blew), can make the same sound. When you're not sure what pattern to use, print the word both ways. Look at the words. Choose the 1 that looks right. It probably is!

Zoom in on Your Words

1. **Highlight Vowel Patterns** Print each Lesson Word. Trace over or underline vowel patterns.

street

2. **Rhyme Time** Find Word Box words that rhyme with the names of these objects.

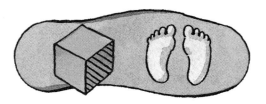

3. **Before Bed** What do you do before "the sun's behind the houses"? Draw a picture of your favourite bedtime activity. Print a sentence to go with your drawing.

4. **Listen Carefully** Trade Lesson Word lists with a partner. Ask your partner to read each word to you. Tell your partner if you hear a **short** or **long vowel** sound, or both.

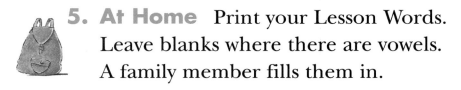

5. **At Home** Print your Lesson Words. Leave blanks where there are vowels. A family member fills them in.

FLASHBACK

What vowel sound do you find easiest to spell?

FOCUS ON LANGUAGE
Expanding Sentences

Read this sentence to a partner.

Tony is wearing a hat.

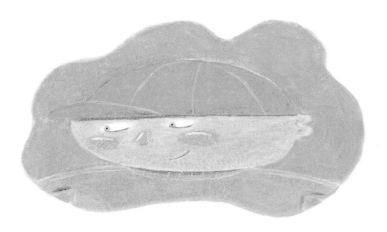

What could you add to this sentence? You could say something about the hat's colour.

Tony is wearing a bright blue hat.

1. Work with a partner. Decide how to expand these sentences.
   a) I like recess.
   b) You have a friend.
   c) I'm going home.

2. Choose a story you have written. Think about how you could expand sentences to make your writing more interesting. Rewrite your story. Share it with a partner.

Would you like to visit Clear Blue Lake Inn?

Word Box

breakfast

great

blend

clean

smile

spill

start

best

Creating Your Word List

Say these words:

What is the same about each of these words?

1. As a class, make a list of words that have blends.

2. Use the Word Box, sign, and class list to make your list of Lesson Words.

3. In your notebook
- Print your Lesson Words.
- Circle the **blend** in each word.
- Add words to your Personal Dictionary.

Strategy Spot

List Your Favourite Strategies

Make a list of your favourite spelling strategies. Put your list in your writing folder or in your Personal Dictionary.

Zoom in on Your Words

1. **Favourites** Use your favourite spelling strategies to learn your Lesson Words.

2. **Make a Word Pyramid**
   Make a pyramid for 3 Lesson Words you want to practise.

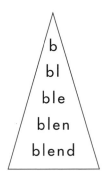

b
bl
ble
blen
blend

3. Find the Word Use Word Box words to complete each group of words. Print the words in your notebook.

       a) _ _ _ _ _ _ _ _ _ , lunch, dinner

       b) _ _ _ _ _, not dirty

       c) good, better, _ _ _ _

       d) big, large, _ _ _ _ _

4. Add the Blend Pick a blend from the basket. Match it with the vowel patterns on the socks. Print words you make.

 5. At Home Make a list of favourite words you learned to spell this year.

FLASHBACK

What is your favourite spelling activity?

124

TECHNOLOGY

Spell Checks

When you write on the computer, use the spell check to proofread your spelling. The spell check will

- highlight words that are not spelled correctly,
- list words that are like your word,
- change your spelling to the correct spelling.

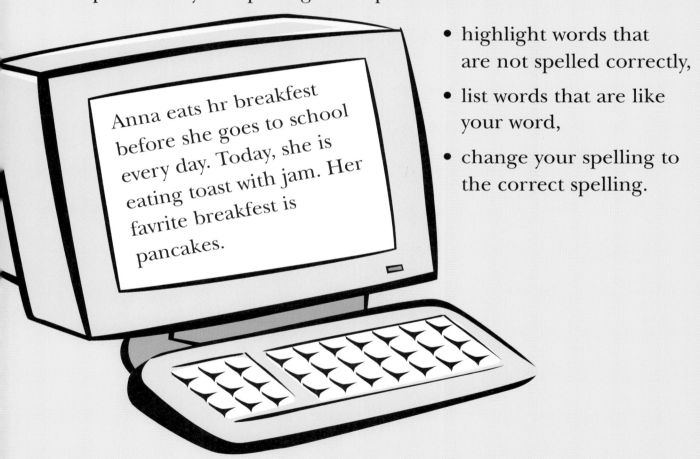

Anna eats hr breakfest before she goes to school every day. Today, she is eating toast with jam. Her favrite breakfest is pancakes.

Imagine that you must do the job of a spell check. Find the spelling mistakes on the screen. Print the correct spelling of the words in your notebook.

Word List

A
about 31
add 3
adding 20
after 21
and 3
at 3
away 13

B
baby 19
ball 26
bed 2
beds 27
bell 26
best 32
big 5
black 9
blend 32
blue 9
boat 16
both 25
box 7
breakfast 32
bring 10
brother 10
brown 10
buy 29
by 29

C
cake 13
cakes 27
call 26

came 13
can't 28
cat 1
child 23
children 23
chin 23
chip 23
chop 23
city 19
class 26
clean 32
clock 9
clown 9
coat 16
come 7
cow 1
cry 19
cut 8
cute 17

D
Dad 2
day 2
did 2
didn't 28
dinner 21
dish 1
dog 1
dogs 27
doing 20
doll 2
don't 28
drum 31

E
each 14
eat 14
eating 20
eye 29

F
fast 3
father 21
fed 4
feed 14
few 17
fill 26
find 15
fine 15
fish 22
five 15
flag 9
flat 9
fly 19
free 14
frog 10
from 10
fun 8

G
game 13
gave 13
get 4
glad 9
glass 9
go 16
going 20
gone 7

got 7
grandfather . 21
grandmother 21
grass 10
great 32
green 10
grow 10

H
hat 3
hats 27
he's 28
helping 20
hide 2
hill 26
him 5
hit 5
home 16
homes 27
hopping 20
hot 7
huge 17
hut 8

I
I 29
I'm 28
I've 28
is 5
it 5